For the Next Earth

For the Next Earth

—— Melissa A. Chappell ——

RESOURCE *Publications* • Eugene, Oregon

FOR THE NEXT EARTH

Resource Publications
An Imprint of Wipf and Stock Publishers
199 W. 8th Ave., Suite 3
Eugene, OR 97401

www.wipfandstock.com

PAPERBACK ISBN: 978-1-7252-9061-7
HARDCOVER ISBN: 978-1-7252-9062-4
EBOOK ISBN: 978-1-7252-9063-1

03/26/21

"Tender Are the Mercies," reprinted with permission
by Alien Buddha Press, May, 2020.

"These Thousand Hills," reprinted with permission
by Borderless Journal, Summer, 2020.

"Among the Lovely Earth," reprinted with permission
by Finishing Line Press., 2019.

"Simple Light," reprinted with permission
by Alien Buddha Pres, 2020.

"After the Storm," reprinted with permission
by Alien Buddha Press, 2020.

For Peter.

For Dustin and Vatsala.

Contents

Acknowledgments

There are so many people who surround me and support me in the work of poetry. My family, Dustin Pickering, Vatsaala Radhakeesoon, The Rev. Dr. David Seymour, the Rev. Ed and Elllen Schaack, Ginni Buller, my new friend Melinda Harmon, Rana Duncan Daston, and so many more whom I have inadvertently overlooked.

I cannot say enough about my therapist, Christine Dowling, who works to keep me grounded like one of the trees which you will so often find in my work.

I would also like to thank the Rev. Steve Jackson and the Rev. Darlene Kelley, who, through their prayer and whose lives are like husks, being cracked open with joy every day, in readiness "for the next earth," I thank them for helping to show the way to both their congregants in dark days.

Thanks to Dustin Pickering, "Famine of the Heart," editor.

Flush with Joy

after "Like the Magic Glow of a Paradise,"
by Clementina Suarez

I have come forth with the young light,

breaking over the waters of the Enoree,

a child of the Daystar.

My poor clay body,

dug from the river,

suddenly the roundness

of flesh.

Eyes are pieces of stained glass,

shattered into a thousand shards

when I was made.

Behold beauty, I tell them.

A throat that sings arias

in crimsons, emeralds, ambers.

Hands that can grasp,

I reach for the Holy One

and pluck a muscadine

from its vagrant vine.

A woman am I,

with hips from which

flow the world,

powerful and ready

for the shattering collide

with the one not yet found.

Legs, ready for the walking,

feet, for the stony road,

to keep moving beyond myself

into the dust of the garden,

where I return again and again—

and again and again

I am raised,

until finally I am broken by my Maker,

and scattered as nourishment for the birds of song.

Rising on wing, I slip earthly bonds into the silvering air,

into the antediluvian, colorless ether, where, flush with joy,

I touch the shimmering face of my Beloved.

Tender Are the Mercies

I walked along with the Sun in the woods today,
droplets of its light winking at me through the limbs,
arms nodding in the breeze.

All of life was rising, after the fierce and holy strife.
The slender blades finding their way,
stretching towards anything above that is blue.

And tender the leaf, having achingly burst forth
from the small bud.
There is pain in the birthing,
but grace in the greening of life.

I lean against the old ash,
where I once took refuge as a child.
Here I was tutored in silence, and patience,
as I sat with the furrowed bark
burrowing into my back,
a blessed woundedness.

I told her of the strivings of humanity,
of the road that we were traveling together,
our bloodied feet, and how imperceivable devastations

were taking our breath away.
Some were withering in their beds,
while others lived to tell.
I told her of the pain,
the improbable places of courage,
and the unbroken sorrowing.

She is still sturdy, and wise.
Quietly she listens, faithfully she hears.
In her silence I hear the unsettled leaves,
the faithful, unseen breath,
and spot some small creature escaping
over the ridge.
I see a cardinal blazing, singing past,
a trail of grace across my wearied eyes.
I caress her bark goodbye,
and look out over the ridge
to the primeval songless rill.

Perhaps the three holy days
did still strive together in me.
Tender is the blade of the word
that can break the red clay of my heart.
Tender are the mercies that heal it.

For the Next Earth

Upon the consequence for Eucharist of Corona 19

They have taken my bread,

because of the tenebrous devastation

that has cast itself all along this earth,

and without it I am a shore without sand,

I am a river without stones.

Without it I starve, fathomless my need.

The body of my Lord, riven in wheat,

buried in deepmost night,

where churns the motions of death,

risen from the soundless tomb,

yet now,

when they have taken my bread,

our Lord is more and more becoming common,

becoming ours, from light to splendid light,

no longer contained by sacred walls

or the studied hands of pastors and priests,

the Christ is free as a fall of water,

a rising dove on the wind,

a heart more spacious than heaven,

yet capable of comprehending my lentil soup,

making his home in the salad from my garden,

allowing himself to be riven in my ordinary bread,

and despite my careless hands,

despite their humility and dishonor,

the Christ, with grace undreamed,

is planted in the furrows of our heart,

a seed for the next earth.

We are the Grass

Our bodies are grass. From the stuff of holiness they come.

At the end of the world, two crossed bars, the lacerated body
    of God, the Son.

Grace bloomed from his wounds, in this tangle of horror.

He was buried in the thick blackness of an earthen cave.

Unbound, he entered the cycle of life infusing it with light, blood,
    life without end.

See how the autumnal victim was buried in the dark loamy earth.

Churning, Turning, Returning, Crushing, all the motions of death.

What can be said about these things? I weep over my mother's bones.

My father's song is silenced. Does life unfold for nothing?

Are we destined for nothing more than holy incineration?

Ashes to ashes, dust to dust. Yet mystery lays hold of us,

In wonder we rake our hands across our eyes,

for the gleaming blade of green breaks through!

It is a blade that slices through our doubting hearts.

It is a blade that wounds us with grace,

for even Jacob left his strivings with God walking with a limp.

But we are the grass, born from the turnings
of the meadows of his heart, growing tender
as mercy, flourishing in his ways,
verdant as the fields of the Lord.

These Thousand Hills

*For the 800,000 people who perished in
the Rwandan genocide of 1994.*

I am a Eucalyptus tree.

For a hundred years I have stood here

with my roots pressed in this Rwandan earth.

They reach down

deep,

deep into the underworld,

where life is not,

and the dead

flee away.

My branches reach

high,

high into the heavens,

where there is

no wrong,

and death

flees away.

But I dwell on earth,

and what I have seen!

What I have seen!

The rain was blood

for my shamed roots,

and loathing myself,

I was made rich

by rotting flesh,

flesh that

no one claimed

because they, too,

had disappeared

into oblivion.

Come, Mercy, come!

Lay an axe to my trunk.

Butcher my wood

as they did the people

to whom I once

gave shade.

Set me ablaze.

Make me a holocaust

to the heavens.

Let me burn!

May my holy essence

float across

these thousand hills

so that none may

be forgotten,

so that none may

be forgotten.

Come, Mercy, come!

Let me burn.

Raise My Head

Darkness too long
upon me,
I must take its indigo
shreds into my own
furrowing wind
and tear it away.
I've been afraid
of the blackbird
that crows every
swarthy fear into being.
Daily he waits
on the fence
for a fissure in my
vulnerable strength.
The fear turns my
crimson flow of blood
from rivers to rivalries.
He comes and seduces,
then cuts me down.
Yet after all these years,
I can hear a thundering beneath
this red clay earth.

It is the green fuse of life that
shall not be broken.
And I shall raise my head,
yes, I shall raise my head,
for the Lord is coming
through the summer wood.

Famine of the Heart

"Lead Us Not into Temptation"

The sky was slate stone,

a famine of tears for Dachau.

The chimneys scraped the heavens,

which refused

the fall of snowy

manna

in those years

when Dachau was a cauldron

of fire and ash.

The ovens burned,

and the ashes fell

over Dachau.

We studied the

hungering ovens,

now starved,

and declared

that we would
never do
such a thing.

We looked at the
gas chamber,
its ceiling outfitted
with gas sprinklers,
and uttered words
of horror at
how this could
happen.

We walked the
demented
barbed wire
walls,
and swore
that we would
never keep humans
in walls of wire.

We all filed into
the visitor's center,
one by one.

We stood in front of a photograph

in monochrome,

of twisted, naked bodies piled high,

barely human.

In the glass we saw a reflection.

It was ours,

hollow eyes

staring back

out of the

depths of horror.

Dachau belongs to humanity:

its ovens,

mouths agape,

we seek out some

residue of ash,

its spyring chimneys,

once the assurance,

both near and far,

that God's people were

suffering a holocaust.

Its gas chamber,

new and unused,

we saw no scratch marks

on the slate gray ceiling,
the barbed wire fence,
impoverished
of butterflies.

Now the famine of tears
slowly began to end
as a soft rain fell from the sky.

Nothing was soft in Dachau.

Not my goodbye.

Not my turned back—
turned,

on the iron words,
forged in eternity:

Arbeit Macht Frei.

Not my blistered thoughts
of other humans going up in flames.

I poured out a libation of tears.

I wept for those who turned to ash.

I wept for myself,

I wept a river, saturating these words

with my compassion,

and my hidden, hungering cruelty.

I left Dachau forever.

Beneath my feet

the broken,

desecrated stones

wept for

Rachel's children,

their remnant

whispers laying bare

humanity's famine of

the heart.

Among the Lovely Earth

I have seen no sign of life

from the carrot seeds that I planted.

They lie beneath,

not taken with the sun,

nor delighting in the shower of water

which I have given them each afternoon.

What lies beneath

is an ache,

a fear of going

where I do not

want to go,

that perhaps the failure

of the seeds was I.

Perhaps the failure

of far greater things

may be claimed by me.

What lies beneath

is a manner of

unsettled pain,

as the earth is unsettled

the first time the plough

is put to its quiet crust,

and cuts a furrow

through what once was content

to be nothing but a field,

fallow for some years,

but now sees the sun

and its burning gaze,

the sage light,

the floating darkness..

What lies beneath is the pain

of wounds healing,

the pain of an old sorrow

being borne away

on a wing of the moon.

At last, at last,

here is the seed,

received into the furrow,

cradled, warm,

among the lovely earth.

Simple Light

A Poem Written on Easter Sunday in Isolation

after "When the Scars Come Out" by Frank G. Honeycutt

I awakened in a simple light
that fell across my shadowed room,
the tormented rudiments that were there
and their razor edges, now gone.
Now just a simple room,
with room enough for simple words:
Blessed be the Beloved,
who has been here, alive,
with lavender on his breath,
and I, I have touched the
wound in his hand,
and this was how I knew him.
And by these marks
we know one another,
where we have been,
where we have died,
and where we have been raised.
We see one another in a simple light,
the light of risen life,
as simple as the sun breaking over the tree line in the morning,
and settling down easy for a first Easter's night.
Like a fiddlehead fern I curl myself, and sleep in his wounds.
O Blessed be the Beloved.
Blessed be Christ.

After the Storm

I awoke to the wind
splitting the vernal air,
raging from the south,
the deep morning howling
like death in chains.

After it was over,
light was poured out
of a broken jar,
as is the most
precious balm,

I walked the yard
to see all that
had been broken.

Then I saw,
sturdily attached
to the limb of the
pin oak,
wound tight
with twigs,
some scrupulous

bird's nest,
bound round in
perfection.
It had been
stripped of nothing
by the stalking wind,
not even one twig.
I peered deep
inside its
hollow dark cavern,
and saw that
it was empty,
the jealous darkness
telling a story of
new life,
somewhere,
heart racing,
blazing in song
across our wearied sight.

Sabbath

I tread the ancient path
this Sabbath day,
to keep it holy.
Holy the dogwood,
virginal, luminescent,
strewn in the woods,
dark, still in
the fight for spring.
We are like the woods,
in their shadowy deeps.
We have been told that
winter is past, yet it
comes with colder winds
and biting air,
coming at us in this time
like a wolf wandering wide
with flesh in his teeth
and blood matting his hair,
prowling the country of humanity.
Is this a day of unrest for the Lord?
Can he not unmake something so
heartless that has been made by some
fluke of genetics?

Is he not God?

He does not hand out answers or solve problems,

and my heart darkens with his mystery.

He is God, and he is restless for his world.

The wolves of the world have crucified him over and over.

They have quarantined him,

had him in lockdown,

had him on ventilators,

taken away his ventilator,

Watched him draw his last breath,

and buried him,

But over and over he is strewn throughout

the darker places of our world

like the virginal, dogwood, tree of light,

a nurse in Spain, giving her last mask to her co worker,

a young woman, in Virginia,

taking food to the homebound,

a pastor, in South Carolina, standing at the ends

of the driveways of shut-ins,

praying for them,

In Italy, arias sung from balconies.

All over the world,

on the penultimate day,

the Lord is restless,

until Spring rises up

like the ocean,

and swallows our

adversary

like the incontestable sea.

And the clouds, brimming

with peace, shall spill

their bounty into

the spring wood.

Then, sublime in his Sabbath,

the Lord will rest easy amongst

the dogwoods,

easy amongst

the dogwoods.

She Wore the Street

She wore the street on her father's army coat.

Her hair was short, but long enough for dreads.

Beaten and beaten, yet back from the dead.

Hope lay in some other city—remote.

Children upon children were love soaked.

Her arms shot up, she was her own worst threat.

Get them. It didn't matter with whom she slept.

Some hours at the Safeway. Too little hope.

On cold nights, as the hem of her blue jeans

drags the street, behold sparks of holiness.

God often comes to us along the seams,

seldom in blazing suns of righteousness.

He lives down in the grime, where streets are mean.

Quiet, he stirs with holy restlessness.

And This is How We Know Him

I have passed beneath the shadows
as I walked round the pathless field.
The long breaking night,
splitting my heart,
I was led by the hand
to the table of heart pine.
So weary was I from
the struggle,
so weary that I fell into a sleep
amongst the dandelions,
a dreamless sleep.
Awakened, a heart opened wide
in a world not my own,
I recalled one breaking open
the bread, earthy, fragrant,
before my eyes,
before the eyes of all those
so weary they could barely
raise their heads,
he is breaking open a new earth,
a new reality strewn with grace
like the boundless constellations of
the great dome of silken night.

He splits apart his own body
for all this pathless world.
And this is how we know
him, whenever bread is broken,
he breaks open his great, oceanic
heart, love rushes into the
world, a rioting river,
into every street corner,
mountain pass, bankrupt store,
devastated hospital.

Broken bread at the evening meal,
there is one here who has traveled
with us from the road.
Broken bread,
broken body.
And this is how we know him.

A Song of Love

On that day when I trespassed into your eyes,

the cedars bowed their heads in contemplation

at the wonder, the astonished joy

that ran rioting through my veins,

to the sea of blessing

that would be shared by us.

Quiet lay the winter,

as did our love.

Yet beneath the holy unbroken crust,

turned the unquiet motions of life.

Happiness was ours the length of those days

as the silvered sun lighted

this space held by two.

Faith lay its hold upon us,

and we trusted that the coming parting

could yet be borne.

We sang through our pain,

and turned to one another

when the green fuse broke the fallow crust,

and the Lord walked the blossoming fields of time.

O How Lovely the Cedars

Let us lie beneath the cedars,
their ancestral dreams peeling away,
falling like scales from the saint's eyes.
Longing to glance the face of God,
they twisted heavenward,
towards a looking-glass sky,
trembling with hope that
the air may be fired with holiness,
so improbable in these latter days,
when even old trees are felled
by the blade for a cut of profit.
Yet knotted and gnarled,
they stand forsaken amongst
the beauty of all other trees.
Even the blade passes them by.

Love, let us lie beneath the cedars,
contriving a bed of evergreen boughs,
and lie gently among them,
their poor branches
giving us shade from the sun,
ardent in its consuming passion for us.

Amongst the cedars,
in our frames racked with desire,
we climb, reaching, together
twisting, turning, touching,
tasting God in the chalice
out of which poured cerulean sky,
yet in your mouth it is wine
that I savor.

Let our rest be among the cedars,
who thought it cursed when in the
looking-glass they saw themselves,
yet God pulsed in the fragrance of
their hungering red hearts.
Together we lie, two felled trees,
knotted in a prayer of thanksgiving
for the storm of fire in our veins
that mirrors the exhaustive,
perishing hunger of the Holy One
for us.

Clear-eyed, him do we see,
one in the other.
I brush the hair from your brow,
as eternity lingers in our mouths,
upon our bed of evergreen boughs.
O how lovely the cedars.

Cadence

Small Graces

I sit down with my lute

of Western Red Cedar and Yew,

I mother it gently into my lap,

its curved back, like the curve of the earth.

My fingers search the courses,

fumbling, breaking the melody

into fractious shards,

the undeniable broken strains

of the world's descant ruptured,

yet dreams of wholeness

blossom in the spaces between,

dreams of daffodils and blue bonnets,

small graces, defying seasons,

blooming along this stony road

that is ours together.